"Hiromi Yoshida racks up more *haijin* cred with her new book of haiku, *Red for Kanreki,* tackling contemporary concerns both personal and global. Still firmly rooted in the American English 5-7-5 tradition, her haiku frequently break the familiar formula of simplicity and deep focus on simple moments in nature. Her playful enjambment wraps around vignettes of daily life as well as reflections on society, paeans to the Beats, and digs at political dorks. *Red for Kanreki* contains a multiverse of experience in many marvelous small packages."

— Tony Brewer, 2024 Indiana Literary Champion, and author of *Water Witch*

Red for *Kanreki*

Haiku by

Hiromi Yoshida

STUBBORN
MULE
PRESS
DEVIL'S ELBOW, MO

Stubborn Mule Press

Devil's Elbow, Missouri

Copyright © Hiromi Yoshida, 2026
First Edition: 1 3 5 7 9 10 8 6 4 2
ISBN: 979-8-89975-028-1
LCCN: 2026934514

Cover image: *Open Arc* by Moya Bligh
Title page image: Toyoko Yoshida
Author photo: Eric Rudd

Acknowledgments

Thanks to Jonathan S Baker and C. S. Matthews for publishing the following haikus in *Icarus Hieroglyph* (The Grind Stone chapbook series, 2023):

"Nostalgia" (under the title "Years"), "winterscape," "Global Warming."

My thanks extend to Emily Bedwell at the Monroe County Public Library for coordinating the 2025 haiku writing contest that I judged.

Thanks, also, to the Writers Guild at Bloomington for so many years of support. Particularly deep thanks to: Tony Brewer, Joan Hawkins, April Ridge, Tyler Frederick, Westley Penland, Molly Gleeson, Antonia Matthew, and James Dorr.

Forever thanks to my mother, Dr. Toyoko Yoshida, without whom none of these years could have happened.

Table of Contents

Bonsai Bloom

Stone Icons

Bonsai Bloom

Japanese Garden

Vermillion carp swish—
beneath hazy pond surface;
Green ripple and sun glint.

Rise

Birds awaken, stir
Ruffled feathers whir to wings
Dappled morning sun.

Awakening

Eggs hatch promises
Of dewy sun-drenched mornings
Hens whir speckled wings.

Seadrift

Sunlit mermaids swim
mourning fallen Icarus
silver piranhas

Nostalgia

The years, wet dervishes,
whirling away, wild-winded,
spin long-haired archives.

Longing

The new year arrives
on wind and rain dripping on
remnant leaves, unraked.

undulate

crows overburden
backyard treetops; raucous sway—
murder of silence.

Weight

crows, sky's black inkblots,
resist windsweep; leave behind
fecal graffiti.

Slipshod

Super moon rising—
silver ghost tangled in trees;
dryads shed green bark.

Silver

ecstasy or fear,
the moon is a wolf tonight
devouring the dark.

Godsmoke

Meat is the substance
Red fleshy animal pulp
The real sacrifice.

Hope

dandelion seed
riding wayward wind-drift—
askew horizons.

Threshold

Dandelion seeds—
Drift in Bloomington twilight,
Promise unkempt bloom.

American Winter

Nationwide deep freeze
Deadly Ohio Turnpike
Soup in homeless hands.

Winter Flow

River surface cracks;
black rocks impede frost flowers
frozen gravity

winterscape

silent snow, two fence
sides, one Zen handclap startles
invisible birds.

Snowdrift

Sheets of snow flying
upward—vapory ghost dance;
black shiver of trees.

Gift

Christmas morning deer
nibbles remnant backyard leaves;
wild antlered wonder.

Slow Spring

March snow, swift madness—
dryads shiver, shed green hair;
trees stretch scrawny arms.

Expectation

Snow dropping from trees
Spring sunlight promises bloom
Dappled dewy grass.

Speck

Snow falling in March—
Winter hangs heavy onto
Shivering grass blades.

Linger

Bloomington snow, so
ephemeral—rabbits leave
no frozen footprints

Luminosity

Snow in March, cold spring;
Bird bath's opaque sediment—
Daffodils shiver.

Sprint

Ephemeral snow
April's fool, trackless green tracts
Rabbit ears quiver.

Into Bloom

April rains pound roofs
black roots; roaring rush of spring—
peony buds crack.

Opacity

Bird wings whir bath glint—
Stir muddy pothole water,
Rainstorm residue.

Summer Evening

green sparks, on, off, on
fiery wind-drift of insect wings
whirring gossamer

Pigment

Bloomington heat wave
scorching Bloomsday predicted;
green roses burning.

Siren

Tornado warning
Hovers in surly storm clouds
Sunday incubus

Sepia Paradise

California burns—
wild acres sprout blackly;
charred carcass eyes glaze.

Fourth of July

Fireworks boom in rain—
Strange onomatopoeia;
Wet branches shiver.

Cycle

desiccated dress;
crinkled cicada remnant—
slip out of green life.

window

sheets of silver rain—
moths, strangely flickering specks;
drowned cicada song.

autumn

maple leaves, red swirl,
rain darkens thirsty grass roots—
fills muddy footprint.

autumn storm

maple leaf windstorm—
spattered window glass shivers;
frenzied dryad tears.

autumn plenitude

November full moon,
treetop pearl undulating;
earth, spitting oyster.

Daylight Saving

Backward fall into
a bed of dead, unraked leaves—
the fugitive hour.

Gravity

Autumn leaves fall on
Hallowed indigenous land;
Buried arrowheads.

Early snow

snowswept November
northward wind stirs remnant leaves—
red cardinal flash.

Remnant

November snowfall
indoor breath clouds window glass—
yellow leaves hang on.

Stone Icons

Beatitude

You, Allen Ginsberg,
illuminating pubic
spaces. Angels burn.

Kingpin

Hey Jack Kerouac,
your Road, a luminous scrawl
through dystopia.

Horizontal

Rambunctious joyride
Neal Cassady on the Road—
Sweaty steering wheel.

Vertical

"Kind king light of mind,"
Jack Kerouac on the Road—
Seamless scroll of words.

Sepia Onomatopoeia

Gary Snyder, you,
beatific Beat remnant,
riprap zen handclap

Ellipsis

Lawrence Ferlinghetti,
City Lights beacon; line break
goes on—beatific.

Breed

Toni Morrison,
laurel tree dryad departs—
colorless eye weeps.

Thicket

Mary Oliver
wandered into word forests—
to return no more.

Stupid Cupid

O Sylvia Plath!
silver dove baked in ovens
charred Valentine thing.

Patty Hearst

That smiling brunette
The camera was her friend
Defying mugshots.

Bloat

The President melts
into a sliver of cheese—
roast the golden calf.

Spit

Obituary:
Rush Limbaugh went out on a limb—
Never to return.

G-String

Kim K. & Kanye West,
Bling fling marriage fizzled out—
Swine ogling fake pearls.

The GOAT

Simone Biles leaping
over hurdles pliantly;
intact sequins glint.

Fish

bell hooks, feminist
theory made arsenal;
brick & mortar dust.

Exit

Martin Luther King
Gunshot cracked the sky open—
His heart, intact star.

Yes

Annunciation
Mary's wan smile, askew veil—
undone handiwork.

Global Warming

The world is burning—
Icarus falling seaward,
The sun, a green coin.

Chinese Breakfast

Fortune cookie bliss
Break me open & access
Stale papered numbers.

F-Word

"fetus" aborted
from CDC lexicons
inane censorship

Road

Freedom ride—bus seats
lumpy; jumpy passengers
squirmed toward storm's eye.

cake walk

grrrl fight revival
no Love for Bikini Kill—
stoke bitch bra bonfires.

Pink

Overworked Cupid—
stupidly fluid arrows—
pretty targets smile.

Tariffed

Iconic Barbie,
Lovely blonde celluloid thing—
Pink resurrection.

Bloated Pinkie

Carrie, YouTube queen,
Barbie's twisted pink sister;
Blood pudding breakfast.

Shard

Columbine gunshots
sprung yellow evidence cards;
cruelest April.

Altar

Día de los Muertos
Uvalde ofrenda weeps—
One black candle stub.

Blink

The dead white woman
Murderer of Emmett Till
A pillar of salt.

Policy

Anti-Asian crimes,
Child's, mother's, purpling bruises—
Turn the other cheek.

Syncopate

BTS, Biden
#StopAsianHate continues
bibimbap & pop.

Unravel

Day of Remembrance
One thousand cranes flyaway—
in paper sunset.

Askew Calligraphy

Mount Fuji blotted
from tourist view—black line,
white void; bad inkbrush—

Umbilical

Detach the mouth from
the wombed site, pearly oyster;
(M)other—break into birth.

Marble

Statue of David
Violates parental rights
Penis dialogues.

Absurdist

Duct-taped banana,
Consuming controversy;
Cryptocurrent thing.

Miles

Fragile bicycles,
Steel frames like the bones of birds;
Icarus speeding—

Crashing the Party

Israel at war;
Hamas shrapnel shift-shapes in
the radical sun.

Promised

Prisoners released—
Palestine, desert mirage;
Gaza, rubble home.

The Choice

Good or Bad Friday,
Flip sides of one tarnished coin;
Barabbas musing.

Easter Sunday

Resurrection is
Insurrection—Jesus smiles,
nailed on stormwashed cross.

Author of two full length poetry collections and six poetry chapbooks, **Hiromi Yoshida** is the Poetry Editor of *Flying Island Journal,* and serves on the board of directors for the Writers Guild at Bloomington, while coordinating the Guild's Last Sunday Poetry reading series. Winner of the Head-to-Head Haiku Battle at the 2022 Granfalloon

Festival, she judged the 2025 Monroe County Public Library haiku writing contest, and leads haiku workshops for the Indiana Writers Center.

This project was made possible, in part, by generous support from the Osage Arts Community.

Osage Arts Community provides temporary time, space and support for the creation of new artistic works in a retreat format, serving creative people of all kinds — visual artists, composers, poets, fiction and nonfiction writers. Located on a 152-acre farm in an isolated rural mountainside setting in Central Missouri and bordered by ¾ of a mile of the Gasconade River, OAC provides residencies to those working alone, as well as welcoming collaborative teams, offering living space and workspace in a country environment to emerging and mid-career artists. For more information, visit us at www.osageac.org

Osage Arts Community

www.ingramcontent.com/pod-product-compliance
Lightning Source LLC
Chambersburg PA
CBHW030606130626
46552CB00006B/2674